HEART FORCE ONE

Abhijit Naskar is the 21st century Neuroscientist who has been serving at the forefront of humankind's struggle against prejudice and discrimination. As an untiring advocate of mental health and global harmony, he became a beloved best-selling author across the world with his very first book "The Art of Neuroscience in Everything". With his revolutionary contributions in Cognitive and Behavioral Neuroscience Naskar has helped the world tackle the horrors of systemic racism, biases, hate and stereotypes more effectively, because of which he is lovingly hailed by humankind as 'the humanitarian scientist'.

HEART FORCE ONE

Need No Gun
to Defend Society

ABHIJIT
NASKAR

Heart Force One:

Need No Gun to Defend Society

Copyright © 2021 Abhijit Naskar

This is a work of non-fiction

An Amazon Publishing Company, 1st Edition, 2021

Printed in the United States of America

ISBN: 9798732706758

Also by Abhijit Naskar

The Art of Neuroscience in Everything
Your Own Neuron: A Tour of Your Psychic Brain
The God Parasite: Revelation of Neuroscience
The Spirituality Engine
Love Sutra: The Neuroscientific Manual of Love
Homo: A Brief History of Consciousness
Neurosutra: The Abhijit Naskar Collection
Autobiography of God: Biopsy of A Cognitive Reality
Biopsy of Religions: Neuroanalysis towards Universal
Tolerance
Prescription: Treating India's Soul
What is Mind?
In Search of Divinity: Journey to The Kingdom of Conscience
Love, God & Neurons: Memoir of a scientist who found
himself by getting lost
The Islamophobic Civilization: Voyage of Acceptance
Neurons of Jesus: Mind of A Teacher, Spouse & Thinker
Neurons, Oxygen & Nanak
The Education Decree
Principia Humanitas
The Krishna Cancer
Rowdy Buddha: The First Sapiens
We Are All Black: A Treatise on Racism
The Bengal Tigress: A Treatise on Gender Equality
Either Civilized or Phobic: A Treatise on Homosexuality
Wise Mating: A Treatise on Monogamy
Illusion of Religion: A Treatise on Religious
Fundamentalism
The Film Testament
Human Making is Our Mission: A Treatise on Parenting
I Am The Thread: My Mission
7 Billion Gods: Humans Above All
Lord is My Sheep: Gospel of Human
Morality Absolute
A Push in Perception
Let The Poor Be Your God
Conscience over Nonsense
Saint of The Sapiens
Time to Save Medicine
Fabric of Humanity
Build Bridges not Walls: In the name of Americana
The Constitution of The United Peoples of Earth

Lives to Serve Before I Sleep
When Humans Unite: Making A World Without Borders
All For Acceptance
Monk Meets World
Mission Reality
Citizens of Peace: Beyond The Savagery of Sovereignty
Operation Justice: To Make A Society That Needs No Law
See No Gender
The Gospel of Technology
Every Generation Needs Caretakers: The Gospel of
Patriotism
Aşkanjali: The Sufi Sermon
Mad About Humans: World Maker's Almanac
Revolution Indomable
When Call The People: My World My Responsibility
No Foreigner Only Family
Hurricane Humans: Give me accountability, I'll give you
peace
Ain't Enough to Look Human
Servitude is Sanctitude
Time To End Democracy: The Meritocratic Manifesto
I Vicdansaadet Speaking: No Rest Till The World is Lifted
Boldly Comes Justice: Sentient not Silent
Good Scientist: When Science and Service Combine
Sleepless for Society
Neden Türk: The Gospel of Secularism
Martyr Meets World: To Solve The Hard Problem of
Inhumanity
The Shape of A Human: Our America Their America
When Veins Ignite: Either Integration or Degradation

DEDICATION

*To the beings of integrity, honor
and accountability.*

CONTENTS

1. Sonnet of Promise

Sonnet of Promise

I made a promise with my life,
Never to leave your side.
How can I maroon you my friend,
When you and I are one light.
Some call me muy loco,
Cause I stand for reason and inclusion.
A world where division is sanity,
Is but a gutter of superstition.
All things have meaning,
When we have people next to us.
Without their presence to fill our life,
Existence is but a futile fuss.
Breathing alone is like choking to death.
A breath shared is a breath well lived.

2. I Am Extremist

There is no handbook to love - there is no handbook to service - for all the teachings that you'll ever require to serve the society – to serve the people – to serve the humankind - are already inside you - all the love is already inside you. Once you figure out your motive, the road will appear itself. Let your motive grasp your whole being - let it spread far and wide through every molecule of yours and envelop you from head to toe.

Let your motive guide your way, not any ideology. Remember, everything is idea, nothing is ideal. Ideal implies flawless and perfect, requiring no correction whatsoever, but idea by nature is flawed and imperfect, that's why it must continue to be scrutinized – that's why it must continue to evolve. An idea demands correction, whereas the ideal demands absolute obedience, and as such, only the idea acts as a gateway to life, whereas the ideal only brings death and destruction. All ideals are anti-life – all ideals are death in disguise.

Nothing in the natural world is in its absolute perfect state. Everything has its flaws, everything has its shortcomings. Only a fool pursues perfection, the wise pursues self-correction. It is only through self-correction can one become less flawed - not perfect mark you, but less imperfect - that is, less animal and more human.

Perfection is an illusion, and when presented as an ideal, it turns out to be a deadly delusion. The loyal and brainless subjects of an ideal are unwilling to accept even the possibility that their beloved ideal could be flawed. Their ideal is their lifeblood, be it a person or a notion, and a threat to that ideal's perfection is a threat to their existence. Thus extremist violence is born.

But here things are not as black and white as they appear. For example, there are two ways to look at the term extremism - one is as an outburst of violence, which is the most accepted and rather predominant definition of extremism, but there is another way to look at the term extremism, that is, an act of revolution - such as the revolution of a nation against oppression. George Washington's fight against the redcoats was such an act of revolution - as such George Washington was an extremist. Likewise, I am an extremist, so is every single being of conscience who has ever tried to lift their thought up the ground against the selfish and rather sectarian norms of society.

When we stand up to oppression, it is not violence, it is revolution - when we stand up to inequality, it is not violence, it is revolution - when we stand up to discrimination, it is not violence, it is revolution. So the question that rises is how does an act of revolution differ from an act of terror or extremist violence? And the answer is, no matter what revolution looked like in the past, violence has no place in a civilized revolution of today - standing up to oppression without harming in return, that is the definition of civilized revolution.

To the civilized revolutionary, such as the BLM protestors, not a single human life is expendable, even that of the oppressor, whereas to the mindless terrorist, such as the Proud Boys, even the loss of innocent lives is acceptable in the pursuit of their mission – in the pursuit of their ideal. But the problem is, we may never have a world with the ideal conditions to practice this principle to the fullest.

We do not live in an ideal world where principles can be practiced without question, we must adapt our principles according to the needs of circumstances. However, excepting the exceptional situation where armed forces are compelled to eliminate a life, which poses a threat to society, or where a civilian accidentally terminates their perpetrator in self-defense, we must live with an incorruptible concern for every human life.

3. Guns Belong to Soldiers, Not Civilians

A society that still needs guns to defend its peace is no different from a bunch of savages with bow and arrow. However, guns are not the problem, the problem is our fetish with guns. And to ensure actual civilized peace, we must destroy this fetish from the very core of our being. War and peace both are manifestations of human will - whatever is your will, so will be the manifestation.

Someone said to me the other day, 'you speak of peace because you are afraid to fight'. I smiled and replied, you are absolutely right, I am terrified of fighting, you know why, because if I raise my hands at someone, there'll be no trace of them left. It's ridiculously easily to take life, especially for a biologist with martial arts training, but what makes a human is the capacity to give life.

Humans are extremely fragile creatures, it doesn't take much to cause them physical harm, but harming someone doesn't say anything about your character - your character is revealed in your desire to help others. In fact, harming others is easy, we've been doing that for millions of years, so have all the other animals on earth.

And this defines very well what the kingdom of the wild is like.

But what is civilization? It is a state of love. When you feel that love towards all humans of planet earth, civilization will be born through each step you take. Defy everything that is not love. When you become love incarnate, civilization will follow. When you become love incarnate, peace will follow. Love is society, hate is jungle.

This doesn't mean there won't be any need for firearms. It may be possible in an imaginary world, but not in a world born in the womb of the wild and spontaneous mother nature. However, if firearms do exist in a civilized society they are to exist only as means to deal with the unrestrainable elements of terror, and that too only by combat units, and not as a force for everyday, personal security. You know why - security brought by guns evaporates fast.

Civilians have a right to firearms no more than they have a right to Uranium-235. The constitution has the luxury to make mistakes, it's just a book - not civilized humans. You see, in the hands of a civilian, a firearm is as dangerous as nuclear weapon. In a functional civilized society built on the premise of peace, guns belong only in the hands of combat personnel, not in the hands of regular civilians, not in the hands of politicians, not even in the hands of billionaires. To put it simply, guns belong to soldiers, not civilians.

This doesn't mean a civilized society has no revolution, in fact, absence of revolution is not a sign of order, it's a sign of conformity to disorder. But a revolution of a civilized society has no place for weapons. Weapons only discredit a revolution. You see, the difference between a revolution and mob rule is that a revolution is run by a drive for ascension, whereas mob rule is governed by sheer nonconformity. Nonconformity is a part of revolution, but it's neither the cause nor the purpose of it.

4. Self-Absorption is Not Empowerment

The civilized human ought to say, my struggle is to end all struggles - my war is to end all wars. I say to you in simple words, if you want to rebel, then rebel for a reason, not just for the sake of rebellion. Those who think, they are cool when they rebel, have no grasp of either revolution or ascension. They are a bunch of aimless ships that try to fill the void in their life through rebellion, like the atheist journalist who used to advocate alcoholism on talk shows or the young entertainer who pretends to be a singer yet acts like an adult performer.

Being famous doesn't relieve a person from accountability, in fact, fame only multiplies the burden of accountability. Because when you are famous, people automatically place you on a pedestal of veneration. Some of these famous nonconformist fools think that by rebelling against the norms of society they are setting an example of empowerment for others, especially the young people, but when a person's rebellion involves nothing but cheap, animal behavior, it's not an act of empowerment, but only an act of degradation - as degrading as the age-old customs of society that these fools so desperately want to defy.

Here one thing that you must remember is, clothes have nothing to do here. Behaving like an empty pervert in a music video or on stage for the young people, doesn't make you a role model of anything, it only legitimizes your sheer shallowness. It is this simple, you can't talk about equality and empowerment by presenting yourself as nothing but a cheap product of gratification. You can't speak up against misogyny by acting as a living misogynistic fantasy of society.

Self-absorption is not empowerment, it's sophisticated barbarism. If you want to use your body as a tool for transformation then use it as a shield against the inequalities in society, rather than fondling your crotch like a coitus-crazed canine. In reforming a society, it's how you behave with your body that counts, not the clothes covering it.

It's with behavior that we'll change the world, not with clothes. Remember, liberty alone won't do, what we need is responsible liberty. You see, liberty is not a new thing, animals live in absolute liberty with no bounds whatsoever since they came to existence on this planet, yet the animal world is not civilized, you know why

– because though they have liberty, they do not have the brain capacity for accountability - and that very absence of accountability makes the kingdom of absolute liberty also the kingdom of absolute cruelty. Hence, it's accountability we ought to focus on, not liberty. And this very accountability will make way for actual civilized liberty, the kind that constitutes a human society and not an animal kingdom.

5. Sonnet of Nonconformity

Sonnet of Nonconformity

Nonconformity is no sign of character,
Nor is swinging on wrecking balls.
Vulgarity is the same as animal liberty,
Only accountability adorns our civilized halls.
Clothes have no bearing on civilization,
Nor does allegiance to law and order.
But habits that endorse self-absorption,
Breed nothing but degradation and disorder.
Perverted animals belong in the jungle,
Self-regulation is vital in civilized society.
If we are to take this world forward,
We must stand tall with honor and sanity.
Naked or not a human is always responsible.
Unregulated freedom sustains a world most cruel.

6. Language of A Human

In a society that is yet to become human, a life of accountability is a life of revolution, for when a strong sense of accountability flows through your veins, it won't let you make any compromise in the face of inhumanity - it's a feeling of an invisible force brewing inside you guiding you in a humane direction every time you are tempted to compromise your humanity. But this is only possible if you make accountability your way of life.

Recklessness of any kind must be thrown away at once. Be observant and if you find anything making you reckless, discard it immediately. Observant and accountable we'll lift the society. I was a good for nothing vagabond roaming the streets of Calcutta. If I have done so much with no resources to speak of, how much will you do! Wake up my friend, the ailing world awaits.

Service is the language of the human in us, selfishness is the language of the animal in us. You are divine when you serve, when selfish you are filth. Let me put it to you plainly – "I am a saint, I must live a saintly life." This is for you to remind yourself from time to time, and not to say to others. But mark you, contrary to popular belief, saintliness doesn't mean flawlessness, saintliness means being aware of the flaws and mending them as you grow through life.

Society needs saints, not the kind manufactured by the filthy factory of the Vatican, but the kind that is human by heart, human by head and human by behavior. Who the hell is the Vatican to declare who is saint and who is not - sacrifice makes a saint, not allegiance to the Vatican. A saint is determined by action and action alone - saintliness is not the possession of any barbaric institution to be endowed on people - saintliness is the plain ordinary drive within each human to become less animal and more human. That is the definition of saintliness - that is the definition of messiahhood - that is the definition of humanitarianism. The criteria for a saint is an untamable desire for sacrifice in the course of serving society, without which all hope for upliftment is bound to dry up in days. Remember, without sacrifice there is no civilization.

Let everyone hear it - you are saint incarnate - you are messiah incarnate - you are humanity incarnate. You are my soldier of ascension, and for a soldier of ascension there is no room for self-gratification, beyond the bare necessities of sustenance. My army is the army without arms - an army of bravehearts radicalized by the mantra of sacrifice in the course of reason, assimilation and ascension.

7. **Army of Lovers**
(The Sonnet)

Army of Lovers
(The Sonnet)

What's needed is an army of lovers,
To set this world on fire,
A fire that burns prejudice to ashes,
And sparks a humanitarian desire.
Lovers devoted to the path of sacrifice,
Pure and chaste serving without reward,
Pursuing the one impossible dream,
The dream of humanizing the entire world.
Not a trace of self within,
Not a kernel of self-obsession,
Uncorrupted and unbending to the bone,
Wake up and be the living ascension.
Drink from the fountain of service effulgent.
Annihilated for others we turn omnipresent.

8. A World Beyond Binary

Forget religion, forget nation, forget ideology - forget every trace of personal identity - forget the religious and non-religious nonsense - forget everything that raises a barrier - forget even your gender. Forget the binary and non-binary nonsense - forget that man and woman nonsense. It is a common human tendency to turn life into a matter of binarism, but life never is binary - diversity is the breath of life.

Just because some idiots can't comprehend any gender other than man and woman, doesn't mean the transgender people don't exist, just like, just because some idiots can't comprehend ideas of progress, except in terms of left and right, doesn't mean the world doesn't exist beyond red and blue.

So, I say again, focus on behavior, not on pronouns. Why you ask? Because gender has no bearing over character. And it is character that makes a society, not gender. Other than in bed, gender has no role in society whatsoever. But mark you, this doesn't mean that we are not to recognize gender - it simply means that a person's gender has no bearing over their functions in society, any more than being left-handed does. We are to recognize gender, we are to make arrangements in society so that people of all gender can live with ease, but we are never to turn the question of gender into a question of character or capacity.

You see, the use of the right pronoun is a step in the right direction, towards atoning for the age-old inability to recognize any gender but male and female, however, it is not the destination - for the ultimate purpose of the struggle for gender fluidity and equality ought to be to turn gender irrelevant in society, not to obsess over it for eternity, just like, the purpose of the struggle for religious harmony is to make religion irrelevant in society, not to obsess over it for eternity. Remember, obsession over gender is as toxic as toxic masculinity.

It is this simple, we don't need a patriarchal society, we don't need a matriarchal society, we just need a human society. And this human society will never become reality so long as we see this world with binary eyes. Computers are binary, not people. All people are non-binary, for life is non-binary. Here by non-binary I am not referring to gender, rather I am referring to non-duality - I am referring to the mental universe that is non-dualistic – that doesn't exist in black and white.

Society has a tendency to look at the world in terms of thesis and anti-thesis - which means, something is either one thing or the other. Popular belief finds it extremely difficult to step across this innate duality and look at life as it is, that is, a manifestation of non-duality. That is why, in the general perception of society, someone is either man or a woman - someone is either believer or an atheist - someone is either capitalist or a socialist - and so on.

But here's the thing, on the road of ascension, duality is but drag. We must leave our duality behind where we leave our fundamentalism. We must rise above the dualities if we are to make any lasting stride in solving real life issues of society. Now the question is why - why must we rise above dualities? It's because, dualities keep us from looking at the whole picture - they keep us from living as whole human beings.

9. Reparations Don't Solve Racism

Influenced by the predominant dualities some people consider systemic racism or slavery to be just a matter of stolen wages. So they argue, can reparations not solve racism! They would if racism was just a matter of stolen wages - it's not, it's a matter of stolen dignity, tranquility and liberty - it's basically a matter of stolen lives. Let me tell you here and now as a black person, we don't expect charity, we just expect the trust and dignity, to which the white person is entitled in this world by default.

If still you don't get the point, let me make it personal for you. Let's say you have a little daughter. One day some wealthy people come to your house and snatch your daughter away from you to make her work as a slave at their place. After twenty years they realize their mistake, so they come to return your now grown-up daughter and they try to compensate for your loss with some money. Now tell me – can any sum of money actually compensate for what you and your daughter lost! The same is with reparations for slavery. A few coins of reparations aren't going to end the inhumanities that people of color continue to face on a regular basis. Reparations can make up for stolen wages, but not stolen dignity and stolen lives.

The problem of systemic racism is much bigger than mere reparations can solve. I am not opposing reparations mark you, but the only thing that can actually make any difference is an everyday, ordinary and yet incorruptible regard for human life in every single person regardless of their color. It is this simple, history can't be changed, but the future starts with our actions today - not just the actions of the colored people, or the gay people, or the women, but of the whole human community. To build an inclusive society, we must first remove color from accountability. The same goes for conscience, the same goes for kindness, the same goes for everything that is human about us.

In short, to build a civilized society, we must overpower the dualities within us and make nonduality a way of life, for as I said, life itself is a manifestation of nonduality. But mark you, here I am not talking about some philosophical nonduality. Nonduality is not a philosophy, nonduality is life. This nonduality has many names - some call it inclusion, some call it unity, some call it oneness, and some others call it wholeness.

And keep in mind, holistic hysteria and healthy wholeness are two different things. The former belongs in the stone-age, the latter in a civilized society. In fact, the very fate of civilization is predicated on wholeness, that is, a plain ordinary sense of oneness - where the human is a whole human being without barriers raised in their psyche tearing them apart from inside out. To put it simply, a whole society is a well society.

10. The Wholeness Sonnet

The Wholeness Sonnet

Free will is not a question of willpower,
It is a question of character.
Civilization is not a question of etiquette,
It is a question of behavior.
Order is not a question of law,
It is a question of accountability.
Harmony is not a question of toleration,
It is a question of inclusivity.
Peace is not a question of diplomacy,
It is a question of nonsectarianism.
Progress is not a question of revenue,
It is a question of collectivism.
When the heart is whole all's well with society.
Fragmentation fills the sky with disparity.

11. Making Democracy Civilized

Where the human is whole, there is peace, where divided, there is war. And today's democracy across the world is founded on the divisiveness of the human psyche. That's why, democracy is not a sign of civilized society, meritocracy is. If people are to choose who runs their lives, then they must first make sure that the options available to them are whole human beings with the capacity to run a society.

Think of medicine for example. You can choose which doctor you want to visit when you need help, but all doctors go through rigorous training to be able to treat a patient. So even if you choose not the best doctor, you can rest assured, you are not going to choose an unskilled doctor, for in the practice of medicine malpractice means loss of license.

And we must treat the practice of politics the same way we treat the practice of medicine. Unskilled politicians have no more place in politics than unskilled doctors have in medicine. And to make sure that only skilled individuals are permitted by law to run for office, we must include training and licensing into our current democratic paradigm. This is the only way forward towards a civilized democracy.

Otherwise democracy will remain a rule of the halfwits, by the halfwits, for the halfwits till kingdom come.

The reason people glorify democracy is that they think if they have the power to choose who runs the affairs of their society, they would have a say in those affairs, which is one of the foul delusions of democracy. People do not have a say in what happens in society, for once a dumbbell is placed in power, they can do whatever they want - you want to believe otherwise, but the practicality of the matter is that, politicians only need people to be placed in power, and once they are elected, that's it - to hell with people - to hell with society. This is not ideal, but this is the reality. And this is the reality of the so-called democracy. So, how do we fix this? As I said, we fix it by making skill and training a mandatory part of politics.

People don't have a say in who gets to become a doctor, yet the practice of medicine continues to be one of the unparalleled wheels of society. So, one wonders why should people have a say in who gets to become a politician? And the answer is, doctors are there to maintain health in the society, they do not determine any other aspect of life of the common citizen, whereas a politician does.

A politician, once placed in power, gains the authority to practically change all aspects of a citizen's life, and that's why, in a civilized society, it is imperative that people decide who gets to determine the affairs of their life - but again, that's not enough - it is not enough for the people to have the power to choose their representative, they must choose a representative with actual capacity. And hard as it may sound, the masses are not capable of distinguishing a capable politician from a crooked dictator.

Therefore, the only way forward is to legislate a training program for interested politicians. And only those who pass the program can run for office, with the license to practice politics as their qualification. And this first revolutionary step from a savage democracy to a civilized democracy can be brought to action, either by a revolutionary politician, or by a revolutionary citizenry. I leave the decision to you.

12. Revolution is Not A Convenience

Revolution never happens because it is acceptable, it happens because everything else turns unacceptable. World War 3 has already begun, but unlike the previous times, it is not a war amongst nations, rather it's a war within nations between the forces of inclusion and reason, and the forces of separatism and superstition. And this World War will continue much longer than the previous two times, for this time, it's a war against the elements of inhumanity within our society, within ourselves, which unlike the previous times, cannot be treated by simply shooting down. Guns kill segregationists, not segregation.

So this time, and now on, the revolution and all the future revolutions must continue without resorting to violence. I am not talking about simply nonviolence, I am talking about having an actual and utter repulsiveness towards violence. This is the fundamental requirement of a civilized revolution. Show strength through your resolve, not through the eagerness for violence. If a terrorist has a gun to your head, don't fight, stare down at them till they drop the gun (metaphorically speaking).

Remember, it ain't just revolution that the world needs, it's civilized revolution, for with time every idea, every thought, every act must evolve. It's not enough to study the evolution of humankind, you must become the next step of evolution. Animals can't, for they don't have the brain capacity to do so, but humans have.

Be the next revolutionary step that defines what humanity ought to look. Don't give in to traditions, be it ideological, political, spiritual or any other. Sharpen yourself, sharpen your thoughts, sharpen your conscience, sharpen your whole perspective of the world - and endow yourself with a vision of a new humanity, and then become the living manifestation of that vision.

13. Civilized Holiness

Break free from the shackles of tradition, and build a new world out of your blood and sweat. Whining about the downfall of the world doesn't undo that downfall. You have to take responsibility yourself. For example, some people try to avoid this responsibility by simply cutting themselves off from society - they call themselves monk, and convinced by some stone-age tradition, they delude themselves with the notion that a monastic life is a holy life, and somehow superior to the life of a household civilian. While it may have held some truth that a monastic life is a holy life, in the olden days, such a life can no longer be considered to be the measure of holiness.

A monk once said to me, 'I live a secluded life in a monastery, and this is the highest form of holiness there is.' I smiled and said, living a secluded life in a monastery, separated from society, is not holiness, it's hysteria. Seclusion doesn't make you holy, kindness does. You see, living a full life, with all its ups and downs, yet being kind to others as family - that's holiness - that's humanity. Churches or monasteries don't make holiness, sacrifice does. I don't visit churches, wherever I stand, becomes a church. I don't live a monastic life, yet I am the very definition of holiness.

It's the shallow who need institutions such as the Church or the Law to tell them what is right, what is wrong, whereas the civilized human is the very epitome of righteousness. That's why I say, I don't obey law, I write them. A civilized human being is the living bible, from which all the institutions of society draw lessons of wholeness, righteousness and humanity.

The civilized human is to become humanity personified. Everything that is civilized, is to be defined by your actions, by your thoughts, by your emotions. There is no other measure of civilization in this world, other than the measure of a civilized heart.

Let me put this into perspective. Once God wanted to learn about holiness. He knocked at my door. This may appear to you as a made-up story, and that is precisely the point - it is indeed a made-up story, so is every such story depicted in scriptures, for as I have said countless times, there is no God, only goodness.

All holiness is born from the civilized heart of the human. Sapiens are the source of all holiness, not some imaginary supreme entity. Sapiens are the source of all sanctity, not some imaginary supreme entity. All the good that is possible in the world, it's because of the humans – all the kindness that is possible in the world, it's because of the humans – all the upliftment that is possible in the world, it's because of the humans.

14. Godless Struggle
(The Sonnet)

Godless Struggle
(The Sonnet)

I don't believe in a God,
That doesn't help the helpless.
Through the history of humankind,
Only humans have served the distressed.
My struggle is to end all struggles,
Says the being of character and conscience.
When you stretch out your hand in love,
That's when civilization manifests.
No help is insignificant,
No kindness is too puny.
With tiny steps we'll humanize the world,
When we see every human as family.
No prayer can heal the troubles of society.
Only cure for degradation is united humanity.

15. Love Above Logic

Everything that is pure, everything that is holy, everything that is inclusive, is born of the human heart. There is no greater force than the force of the heart. Till the heart engulfs the whole society, no head, no science, no logic can elevate the world.

I am a scientist, so of course I hold nothing back to say out loud, science is a peerless force for good, but a little knowledge of science is dangerous, it makes you cynical towards anything that is not logical. Life can't be lived on logic alone. Logic has its place surely, but logic is not the lifeblood of civilization. Not everything that is civilized is logical, and not everything that is logical is civilized.

Let me elaborate. Love knows no logic, yet without it, there is no life. Life without some logic is a stone-age existence, but life without love is no existence. Here some half-educated intellectual may argue, love is logical, for it leads to reproduction thus ensuring survival. To which I have only one thing to say - those who analyze love as a task of biology or intellect, don't know a single thing about love.

Their understanding is but a half-baked cookie - worth nothing. On the other hand, one who knows where to practice logic and where sentiment, is the true sage on the face of earth. Such human doesn't love, they are love itself - such human doesn't know, they are knowledge itself - such human doesn't exist, they are existence itself.

No matter how high this human flies, they are always grounded in the soil - they are always tethered to society. When you lose touch with soil and society, you lose touch with life, for a life without soil is a life without roots and a life without society is a life without sweetness.

So breathe deeply in the purifying aroma of the soil, and serve the society with every drop of life in your veins. This is my command to all the Naskareans in the world - I do not want followers of Naskar, I want servants of humanity - give up the self to lift the society, and that would be your greatest gift to me. Every Naskarean ought to be the 911 to society. What have you to fear my soldier - you are a reflection of Naskar - you are humanity personified.

It is a troubled reality that we live in, and to change that we have to take responsibility for that reality, instead of hoping that some invisible force from the Vatican or the Capitol will fix it for us. We are the solution and we must live as such. Be the answer to the questions that google can't solve.

The existence of government doesn't mean civil liberation from accountability. In fact, a nation can run without government, but it can't run without the accountability of its citizens. Government is merely one thread upon the vast fabric of civilization. And the integrity of this fabric is predicated on the integrity of the everyday, ordinary human beings - it is predicated on the accountability of the everyday, ordinary human beings - of you, of me, of each one of us.

16. The Naskarean Sonnet

The Naskarean Sonnet

It ain't easy to get Naskar,
For Naskar is no being binary.
In a world full of dualities,
Naskar is an emblem of inclusivity.
Think not it to be a person,
For the person perished in line of duty.
What lives today is the idea,
The idea of struggle for undivided amity.
Every human who helps a human,
Is a manifestation Naskarean.
Wherever there is prejudice and inequality,
They appear as a living revolution.
When one Naskar dies a thousand will rise.
The dream of unity will never face demise.

17. Making Britain Civilized

Some dumbbells believe politicians as the measure of civilization - some believe celebrities as the measure of civilization, so let me put it straight, the measure of civilization is character and character alone, for a being of character is a being with accountability, and a being with accountability is the foundation of civilization.

Let me give you an example. Think of the British empire. Despite the irreparable atrocities committed by them, there are still many British who actually take pride in their ancestors' barbaric escapades across the world, without the slightest bit of remorse, let alone accountability. Those horrors cannot be undone, and no reparations can repair the horrors faced by the people subjugated by the imperialist savages, but even in this day and age, if the modern British do not have some sense of accountability for those actions of the past, then they are not modern humans to begin with, but merely an uncivilized bunch.

If only you could see the British empire with the same eye as you see the Nazis, then you'd realize that the human rights violations committed by the British barbarians outnumber those of the Third Reich. You vilify Hitler yet glorify Buckingham Palace, when the atrocities of the palace far outweigh the atrocities of Hitler. Hitler tortured people in Germany, whereas the British empire tortured people all around the world - in South Africa, in India, in Australia - the list just continues. If Adolf Hitler was a manifestation of the worst of human nature, so was, and still greatly is, Britain, that is, the monarchy and its loyal, spineless subjects. Therefore, it's time we stop using the terms Great and Britain side by side.

Almost every nation has committed atrocities at one time or another, and turning a blind eye to them won't make that nation civilized, what will is the willingness to take responsibility, because only when we take responsibility of the errors committed in the past can we wholeheartedly devote ourselves to never repeat those errors every again. And in this respect, the British seem to be moving in exactly the opposite direction, that is, in the primitive direction of glorifying the heinous past, and not in the civilized direction of accountability.

Nothing civilized is ever produced without accountability. You see, I don't have any dumb patriotic loyalty to any particular nation, so I do not have the desire, either conscious or subconscious, to impress any particular nation. I belong to the whole world, and every nation in it is my responsibility. Yes America is my homeland, for she adopted me when nobody knew I existed, but no one nation is superior to me than the rest. No government is my authority, no monarchy is my master. I am here to civilize the governments and abolish the monarchies.

I could say, I am here to abolish the governments as well, but I cannot in right conscience - you know why - because society will continue to need some form of government for a long time - but it ought to be a government of merit and character, not of popularity and superstition. If a government is born of merit and character, they would not need pressure from humanitarians and activists to reform its out-of-date policies - they would do it on their own, because they are accountable.

For example, if Britain ever had an actual government of merit and character, it would have severed all ties with the stone-age system of monarchy long time ago. A truly civilized government would activate reforms in all parts of society as soon as it comes to power, such as the Biden-Harris administration. Reform is not a question of capacity, it's a question of willingness.

18. The British Sonnet

The British Sonnet

Rule Britannia,
Britannia rule the waves.
Britons never, never, never,
Shall be slaves.
Around the world we looted,
We even championed slavery.
But none of it really matters,
Consequences don't apply to royalty.
Hitler massacred so many people,
Which is petty compared to our atrocities.
Perhaps that's why Britain is so great,
None can compete with our killing spree.
It's time to civilize this backward Britannia,
By righting the wrongs of British Barbariana.

19. When Calls The South

To be willing to change, one has to acknowledge the follies. But if you do not even see the follies as follies, how will you change? And no reason in the world can change such a heart, for it is not a heart, but an active vessel of prejudice. Take the south for example. A great many people in the south (not all) still see nothing wrong in the confederate history of America, in fact, they take pride in it, and do everything in their power to bring that history back to life.

To these white supremacists, be it in the south or elsewhere in our country, or indeed anywhere in the world, equality is a satanic concept, for only the white people are God's chosen people and all other people as well as animals are there to serve a life of slavery for the white people. So, the question is, how can you reason with such stone-age beliefs? The answer is, you can't.

But at the same time, you can't force them with violence to change their belief, for if you do that, then you'd be no better than them. Therefore, the only way forward is, stick to your conviction of equality, inclusion and acceptance, and when you see those savages doing harm to others, restrain them, like you'd restrain a bully – you don't harm a bully, but you don't let them do whatever they want either.

If country-life can't be the very epitome of warmth and acceptance, then such life is not worth a single ounce of glory we usually bestow upon it. Horses, boots and hats don't constitute country life, humility, simplicity and compassion do. People from the country ought to be at the forefront of humankind's struggle for kindness and equality, and yet, the situation is quite the opposite. They say, people shouldn't come from other nations to America in the hope of life and liberty, because America is the white people's nation. To them I say, unless you are an American Indian, you are a descendant of an immigrant yourself, so before asking someone else to leave the nation, you should leave first.

You see, if we go back in time long enough, then other than the Africans living in Africa, everybody on earth is a descendant of immigrants who migrated to various parts of the world from humankind's original homeland Africa. However, it is of no use to reason with the white supremacists, and it'll be even more foolish to assume that they'll see the light of humanity sooner or later. But I can assure you this, if you can continue the struggle for humanity, sooner or later the future descendants of these supremacist savages will turn human. So I repeat again, this is my commandment to you – restrain the oppressor, don't harm them.

20. The Country Sonnet

The Country Sonnet

I stand beneath the southern sky,
Looking up at the heavenly bodies.
The twinkling stars know no color,
Then why we mortals beneath act so puny!
Country means heart, country means humility,
All that is pure is born in the country.
How could we poison its innocent soul,
By our savage escapades of bigotry!
It's high time we be the example of kindness,
For the streams of Mississippi carry acceptance.
Behold ye all blind with confederate pride,
Conscience rises above the Blue Ridge Mountains.
Let's resuscitate the country with love and passion.
We'll turn this land into a cradle of amalgamation.

21. The Making of Peace

If we are to create an actual society of peace and integration, then we must, from now on, stop resorting to violence every time we come across some difficulty. We must think love, dream love, live love - and that too, not out of compulsion, but out of accountability. Because only if we could dedicate ourselves genuinely through centuries to the making of peace, there will rise the actual possibility of peace - only then there'll be actual manifestation of integration - otherwise, there'll only be talks of integration and harmony, not actual integration and harmony.

Integration is unity, unity is ascension. Let me put it another way. Another name for sectarianism is extinction. In a civilized world there is no greater force than assimilation - assimilation overpowers prejudice as well as intellectual argumentation, leaving no room for hate. Prejudice is the prelude to war, assimilation is the cure.

People have a tendency to see prejudice as lack of intellect, but in reality, prejudice comes in all forms - there's prejudice that is sustained by the lack of intellect or knowledge, but there's also another kind of prejudice that is sustained by intellect. Intellect has no conscience of its own - it knows not the meaning of humanity. That's why, a person can be the most intellectual creature on earth, yet be an animal in disguise, but a person of assimilation can never be an animal.

Let everyone hear it, I do not want peace and harmony, I want accountability and assimilation, for when there are accountability and assimilation, peace and harmony will follow. Peace and harmony are not the act, they are the result - they are the result of everyday ordinary human acts of accountability and assimilation.

22. Sonnet of Human Intervention

Sonnet of Human Intervention

Vegetables often say,
In the end all will be well.
It is but an illusion of control,
Progress comes not through silent spell.
Nothing good happens by magic,
Every good requires human intervention.
When we stand up and act with conscience,
Only then we'll cause real ascension.
The whole world is my responsibility,
Thus speaks the civilized human.
Defy the norm that makes you selfish,
Embodying love's enduring aspiration.
Forget not, we are but each other's keeper,
Born not to be intellectual, but drunken lover.

23. Labor of Heart

The earth is humanized by heroes - be a hero my friend - always say, I am responsible, I am accountable, I am invincible. None can solve the hard problem of inhumanity, you have to solve it from inside out. Neither name, nor money, nor intellect will lift this world, only character will. Character can pierce through the dark night of inhumanity and herald the advent of the humane dawn. Remember, light can stand all darkness, but darkness cannot stand even a trace of light.

When it is dark, keep working - when there is light, still keep working. Do not go throwing others under the bus - if not the whole world, take the responsibility of your neighborhood on your shoulders. They alone live, who live with responsibility, others merely crawl.

Never you say, you can do nothing for the world, for you are a puny mortal. You are all Gods, sin is to call you puny mortals. An animal is born to follow nature, a human is born to conquer it. Stand up and announce the humanity within you. Everything can be sacrificed for humanity, humanity can be sacrificed for nothing.

The road to a civilized world, founded on humanity, is the labor of the heart, not of the head - head is to serve in that course, but not to be the master. Humanity - humanity - humanity - this should be on your mind 24/7, only then will the world around you turn human.

There is nothing outside the mind, neither humanity nor inhumanity - so, once you conquer the inhumanity in your mind, the humanity within will be radiated outside. Search for humanity, you'll find only yourself - search for yourself, you'll find only humanity. Convert none, help all.

Like a bubble in water, the civilized human rises, exists and dissolves in the people. This is the gist of a religious life - this is the gist of a civilized life - this is the gist of a human life. Don't try to bring anyone down to your knee, lift everyone up above your head.

24. Shake The World Savaşçı
(The Sonnet)

Shake The World Savaşçı
(The Sonnet)

Shake the world savaşçı,
The world is only a reflection of you.
Break the mold o kahraman,
In a civilized time these molds won't do.
Your story is the one of a warrior,
Not the one fighting with weapon.
You are the hero without arms,
Your power is your determination.
One person can end a war,
If they give all to the making of peace.
You are the answer to the world's prayers,
But you must keep your prejudice on leash.
Go sleepless, starving and unappraised if needed.
Be the guerra of inclusion and unite the divided.

(savaşçı = warrior, kahraman = hero, guerra = war/struggle)

25. No Revolution, Only Life

Love alone triumphs, not intellect, not prejudice - love alone. All things perish, intellect, faith, superstition - not love. The superstitious never lives, the intellectual may live a little, but the being of love never dies. Whatever exists can exist either as an instrument of love, or nothing at all.

That person reaches immortality who can give all for love without reserve, without insecurity, without expectation. Time is short - there is no time for debate - no time for argumentation - take up one idea and live that idea, with your last ounce of courage. Live your life as the emblem of an impossible dream.

Everybody can walk where there is a path, greatness is to walk without a path and leave a trail for others. Don't teach, live your life as a living teaching for all humanity - be a living revolution. You see, there is no revolution, there is only life. Society calls it revolution, because they think of life to be something constant, and any change to be revolutionary. Life itself is the manifestation of change - it is the manifestation of evolution - either it evolves or perishes.

Society doesn't progress by chanting some prayers - you must become the answer to those prayers. Those who are dead, pray. Those who are alive, do. That's how a society moves ahead - that's how a species moves ahead. I have no grudge against the lifeless corpses, but it's from the alive humans that my soldiers will come - soldiers capable of moving mountains - soldiers capable of breathing life into the barren desert - these unbending, unafraid, uncorrupted soldiers, bearing unbearable pain, will lift the world from the ashes of darkness up into the civilized dawn.

BIBLIOGRAPHY

Archer M., (2000), Being Human: The Problem of Agency. Cambridge University Press.

Archer M., (2003), Structure, Agency and the Internal Conversation. Cambridge University Press.

Adolphs R (2003) Cognitive neuroscience of human social behaviour. Nature Rev Neurosci 4: 165–178.

Adolphs R, Tranel D, Damasio AR (2003) Dissociable neural systems for recognizing emotions. Brain Cogn 52: 61–69.

Afton, A. D. (1985). Forced copulation as a reproductive strategy of male lesser scaup: A field test of some predictions. - Behaviour 92, p. 146-167.

Allison T, Puce A, McCarthy G. (2000) Social perception from visual cues: role of the STS region. Trends Cogn Sci 4: 267–278.

Andresen, Jensine, and Robert Forman, eds. Cognitive Models and Spiritual Maps. Bowling Green, Ohio: Imprint Academic, 2000.

Ashbrook, James, and Carol Albright. The Humanizing Brain: Where Religion and Neuroscience Meet. Cleveland, OH: Pilgrim Press, 1997.

Azari, Nina, Janpeter Nickel, Gilbert Wunderlich, Michael Niedeggen, Harald Hefter, Lutz Tellmann, Hans Herzog, Petra Stoerig, Dieter Birnbacher, and Rudiger Seitz. "Neural Correlates of Religious Experience." European Journal of Neuroscience 13, no. 8 (2001)

Agar, N. (2004). Liberal eugenics: In defence of human enhancement. London: Blackwell Publishing.

Alteheld, N., Roessler, G., Vobig, M., & Walter, R. (2004). The retina implant new approach to a visual prosthesis. Biomedizinische Technik, 49(4), 99–103.

Antal, A., Nitsche, M. A., Kincses, T. Z., Kruse, W., Hoffmann, K. P., & Paulus, W. (2004a). Facilitation of visuo-motor learning by transcranial direct current stimulation of the motor and extrastriate visual areas in humans. European Journal of Neuroscience, 19(10), 2888–2892.

Bhat Z, Kumar, S, Bhat H (2015) In vitro meat production. Challenges and benefits over conventional meat production. J Sci Food Agric 14: 241–248

Bernstein R. J., (1967), John Dewey. New York: Washington Square Press.

Bernstein R.J., (1971), Praxis and Action: Contemporary Philosophies of Human Activity. Philadelphia: University of Pennsylvania Press.

Bernstein R.J., (1976), The Restructuring Social and Political Thought.

Bernstein R.J., (1983), Beyond Relativism and Objectivism: Science, Hermeneutics, and Praxis. Philadelphia: University of Pennsylvania Press.

Bernstein R.J., (1986), Philosophical Profiles. Philadelphia: University of Pennsylvania Press.

Bernstein R.J., (1991), New Constellation. Cambridge: MIT Press.

Barash, D. P. (1977). Sociobiology of rape in mallards (Anas platyrhynchos): Responses of the mated male. - Science 197, p. 788-789.

Berger, J. (1986). Wild horses of the great basin: Social competition and population size. - The University of Chicago Press, Chicago.

Birkhead, T. R., Johnson, S. D. & Nettleship, D. N. (1985). Extra-pair matings and mate guarding in the common murre Uria aalge. - Anim. Behav. 33, p. 608-619.

Beauregard, Mario, and Vincent Paquette. "Neural Correlates of a Mystical Experience in Carmelite Nuns." Neuroscience Letters 405, no. 3 (2006)

Benson, Herbert. Timeless Healing: The Power and Biology of Belief. New York: Scribner, 1996

Bose, Subhas Chandra. An Indian Pilgrim: An Unfinished Autobiography, Oxford University Press, 1997

Bose, Subhas Chandra. The Indian Struggle 1920-1942, Oxford University Press, 1997

Bogen, J.E.(1995a), 'On the neurophysiology of consciousness:

Part I. An overview', Consciousness and Cognition, 4.

Bogen, J.E. (1995b), 'On the neurophysiology of consciousness: Part II. Constraining the semantic problem', Consciousness and Cognition, 4.

Bremner, J. D., R. Soufer, et al. (2001). "Gender differences in cognitive and neural correlates of remembrance of emotional words." Psychopharmacol Bull 35 (3).

Brothers, L. (2002). The social brain: A project for integrating primate behavior and neurophysiology in a new domain. In J. T. Cacioppo et al. (Eds.), Foundations in neuroscience. Cambridge, MA: MIT Press.

Buss, D. D. (2003). Evolutionary Psychology: The New Science of Mind, 2nd ed. New York: Allyn & Bacon.

Buss, D. M. (1989). "Conflict between the sexes: Strategic interference and the evocation of anger and upset." J Pers Soc Psychol 56 (5).

Buss, D. M. (1995). "Psychological sex differences. Origins through sexual selection." Am Psychol 50 (3).

Buss, D. M. (2002). "Review: Human Mate Guarding." Neuro Endocrinol Lett 23 (Suppl 4).

Buss, D. M., and D. P. Schmitt (1993). "Sexual strategies theory: An evolutionary perspective on human mating." Psychol Rev 100 (2).

Blakemore SJ, Decety J (2001) From the perception of action to the understanding of intention. Nature Rev Neurosci 2: 561.

Bruce C, Desimone R, Gross CG (1981) Visual properties of neurons in a polysensory area in superior temporal sulcus of the macaque. J Neurophysiol 46: 369–384.

Buccino G, Vogt S, Ritzl A, Fink GR, Zilles K, Freund HJ, Rizzolatti G (2004) Neural circuits underlying imitation of hand actions: an event related fMRI study. Neuron 42: 323–34.

Colapietro V., (1988), "Human Agency: The Habits of Our Being." Southern Journal of Philosophy, XXVI, 2, pp. 153-68.

Colapietro V., (1992), "Purpose, Power, and Agency." The Monist, 75, 4 (October) pp. 423-44.

Colapietro V., (2003), "Signs and their vicissitudes: Meanings in excess of consciousness and functionality." Logica, Dialogica, Ideologica, a cure di Susan Petrilli e Patrizia Calefato (Milano: Mimesis), pp. 221-36.

Colapietro V., (2004a), "C. S. Peirce's Reclamation of Teleology." Nature in American Philosophy, ed. Jean De Groot (Washington, D.C.: Catholic

University Press of America), pp. 88-108.

Colapietro V., (2004b), "Portrait of a Historicist: An Alternative Reading of Peircean Semiotic." Semiotiche, 2/04 [maggio 2004], pp. 49-68.

Colapietro V., (2006), "Engaged Pluralism: Between Alterity and Sociality." The Pragmatic Century: Conversations with Richard J. Bernstein (Albany, NY: SUNY Press), pp. 39-68.

Colapietro V., (2009), "Habit, Competence, and Purpose." Forthcoming in The Transactions of the Charles S. Peirce Society. Calder AJ, Keane J, Manes F, Antoun N, Young AW (2000) Impaired recognition and experience of disgust following brain injury. Nature Neurosci 3: 1077–1078.

Carey DP, Perrett DI, Oram MW (1997) Recognizing, understanding and reproducing actions. In: Jeannerod M, Grafman J (eds) Handbook of neuropsychology. Vol. 11: Action and cognition. Elsevier, Amsterdam.

Carr L, Iacoboni M, Dubeau MC, Mazziotta JC, Lenzi GL (2003) Neural mechanisms of empathy in humans: a relay from neural systems for imitation to limbic areas. Proc Natl Acad Sci USA 100: 5497–5502.

Changeux JP, Ricoeur P (1998) La nature et la règle. Odile Jacob, Paris.

Cochin S, Barthelemy C, Roux S, Martineau J (1999) Observation and execution of movement: similarities demonstrated by quantified electroencephalograpy. Eur J Neurosci 11: 1839– 1842.

Chomsky Noam, (2017) Requiem for the American Dream

Chomsky Noam, (2016) Who Rules the World?

Chomsky Noam, (2010) How the World Works

Churchland, P.S. (1986), Neurophilosophy (Cambridge, MA: The MIT Press).

Churchland, P.S. & Ramachandran, V.S. (1993), 'Filling in: Why Dennett is wrong', in Dennett and His Critics: Demystifying Mind, ed. B. Dahlbom (Oxford: Blackwell Scientific Press).

Churchland, P.S., Ramachandran, V.S. & Sejnowski, T.J. (1994), 'A critique of pure vision', in Large- scale Neuronal Theories of the Brain, ed. C. Koch & J.L. Davis (Cambridge, MA: The MIT Press).

Crick, F. (1994), The Astonishing Hypothesis: The Scientific Search for the Soul (New York: Simon and Schuster).

Crick, F. (1996), 'Visual perception: rivalry and consciousness', Nature, 379.

Crick, F. & Koch, C. (1992), 'The problem of consciousness', Scientific American, 267.

Craig AD (2002) How do you feel? Interoception: the sense of the physiological condition of the body. Nature Rev Neurosci 3: 655–666.

Damasio, A (2003a) Looking for Spinoza. Harcourt Inc. Damasio A (2003b) Feeling of emotion and the self. Ann NY Acad Sci 1001: 253–261.

d'Aquili, Eugene. "Senses of Reality in Science and Religion." Zygon 17, no 4 (1982)

d'Aquili, Eugene. "The Biopsychological Determinants of Religious Ritual Behavior." Zygon 10, no. 1 (1975)

d'Aquili, Eugene. "The Myth-Ritual Complex: A Biogenetic Structural Analysis." Zygon 18, no. 3 (1983) d'Aquili, Eugene, and Andrew Newberg. The Mystical Mind: Probing the Biology of Religious Experience. Minneapolis: Fortress Press, 1999.

Daly DD. 1958. Ictal affect. Am J Psychiatry.

Damasio, A. (1994) Descartes' Error: Emotion, Reason and the Human Brain. New York, Putnams.

Damasio, A. (1999) The Feeling of What Happens: Body, Emotion and the Making of Consciousness. London, Heinemann.

Darwin, C. (1859) On the Origin of Species by Means of Natural Selection. London, Murray.

Darwin, C. (1871) The Descent of Man and Selection in Relation to Sex. London, John Murray.

Darwin, C. (1872) The Expression of the Emotions in Man and Animals. London, John Murray; also published

1965, Chicago, University of Chicago Press.

Dawkins, M.S. (1987) Minding and mattering. In C. Blakemore and S. Greenfield (eds) Mindwaves. Oxford, Blackwell, 151-60.

Dawkins, R. (1976) The Selfish Gene. Oxford, Oxford University Press; a new edition, with additional material, was published in 1989.

Dawkins, R. (1986) The Blind Watchmaker. London, Longman.

Di Pellegrino G, Fadiga L, Fogassi L, Gallese V, Rizzolatti G (1992) Understanding motor events: A neurophysiological study. Exp Brain Res 91: 176–80.

Deikman, A.J. (2000) A functional approach to mysticism. Journal of Consciousness Studies 7(11-12), 75-91.

Delmonte, M.M. (1987) Personality and meditation. In M. West (ed.) The

Psychology of Meditation. Oxford, Clarendon Press, 118-32.

Dennett, D.C. (1987) The Intentional Stance. Cambridge, MA, MIT Press.

Dennett, D.C. (1988) Quining qualia. In A.J. Marcel and E. Bisiach (eds) Consciousness in Contemporary Science. Oxford, Oxford University Press, 42-77.

Dennett, D.C. (1991) Consciousness Explained. Boston, MA, and London, Little, Brown and Co.

Dennett, D.C. (1995a) Darwin's Dangerous Idea. London, Penguin.

Dennett, D.C. (1995b) The unimagined preposterousness of zombies. Journal of Consciousness Studies 2(4), 322-6.

Dennett, D.C. (1995c) Cog: steps towards consciousness in robots. In T. Metzinger (ed.) Conscious Experience. Thorverton, Devon, Imprint Academic, 471-87.

Dennett, D.C. (1995d) The path not taken. Behavioral and Brain Sciences 18, 252-3; commentary on N. Block, On a confusion about a function of consciousness. Behavioral and Brain Sciences 18, 227.

Dennett, D.C. (1996a) Facing backwards on the problem of consciousness. Journal of Consciousness Studies 3(1), 4-6.

Dennett, D.C. (1996b) Kinds of Minds: Towards an Understanding of Consciousness. London, Weidenfeld & Nicolson.

Dennett, D.C. (1997) An exchange with Daniel Dennett. In J. Searle (ed.) The Mystery of Consciousness. New York, New York Review of Books, 115-19.

Dennett, D.C. (1998) The myth of double transduction. In S.R. Hameroff, A.W. Kaszniak and A. C. Scott (eds) Toward a Science of Consciousness: The Second Tucson Discussions and

Debates. Cambridge, MA, MIT Press, 97-107.

Dennett, D.C. (1998b) Brainchildren: Essays on Designing Minds. Cambridge, MA, MIT Press.

Dennett, D.C. (2001) The fantasy of first person science. Debate with D. Chalmers, Northwestern University, Evanston, IL, February 2001.

Dennett, D.C. (2003) Freedom Evolves. New York, Penguin.

Dennett, D.C. and Kinsbourne, M. (1992) Time and the observer: the where and when of consciousness in the brain. Behavioral and Brain Sciences 15, 183-247, including commentaries and authors' responses.

Dewey J., (1911 [1977]), "Epistemological Realism: The Alleged Ubiquity of the Knowledge Relation." Journal of Philosophy, VIII, 20 (September 28, 1911).

Dewhurst, Kenneth, and A. W. Beard. "Sudden Religious Conversions in Temporal Lobe Epilepsy." British Journal of Psychiatry 117 (1970)

Dewhurst K, Beard AW. Sudden religious conversions in temporal lobe epilepsy. 1970 Epilepsy Behav 2003

Devinsky O, Lai G. Spirituality and religion in epilepsy. Epilepsy Behav 2008.

Devinsky, O., Morrell, MJ, Vogt, BA. (1995) 'Contribution of anterior cingulate cortex to behavior', Brain, 118.

Douglas Stone A., Chapter 24, The Indian Comet, in the book Einstein and the Quantum, Princeton University Press, Princeton, New Jersey, 2013.

E. Horvitz, "One Hundred Year Study on Artificial Intelligence: Reflections and Framing," ed: Stanford University, 2014.

Einstein A. (1925). "Quantentheorie des einatomigen idealen Gases". Sitzungsberichte der Preussischen Akademie der Wissenschaften.

Eckhart Meister, Selected Writings

Egidi R., ed. (1999), "Von Wright and 'Dante's Dream': Stages in a Philosophical Pilgrim's Progress", in In Search of a New Humanism: the Philosophy of G.H. von Wright, ed. by R. Egidi, Kluwer, Dordrecht.

Fadiga L, Fogassi L, Pavesi G, Rizzolatti G (1995) Motor facilitation during action observation: a magnetic stimulation study. J Neurophysiol 73: 2608–2611.

Fogassi L, Gallese V, Fadiga L, Rizzolatti G (1998) Neurons responding to the sight of goal directed hand/arm actions in the parietal area PF (7b) of the macaque monkey. Soc Neurosci Abs 24:257.5.

Frith U, Frith CD (2003) Development and neurophysiology of mentalizing. Philos Trans R Soc Lond B Biol Sci 358: 459.

Farah, M.J. (1989), 'The neural basis of mental imagery', Trends in Neurosciences, 10.

Finlay BL, Darlington RB (1995) Linked regularities in the development and evolution of mammalian brains. Science 268.

Freud, S. "The Interpretation of Dreams", 1900

Freud, S. "Selected papers on hysteria and other psychoneuroses" Journal of Nervous and Mental Disease 1909.

Freud, S. "The Origin and Development of Psychoanalysis", 1910

Freud, S. "Psychopathology of everyday life", 1914

Freud, S. "Beyond the Pleasure Principle", 1920

Frith, C.D. & Dolan, R.J. (1997), 'Abnormal beliefs: Delusions and memory', Paper presented at the May, 1997, Harvard Conference on Memory and Belief.

Gay, Volney, ed. Neuroscience and Religion. Plymouth, UK: Lexington Books, 2009.

Gazzaniga, M. S. (1985). The social brain. New York: Basic Books.

Gazzaniga, M.S. (1993), 'Brain mechanisms and conscious experience', Ciba Foundation Symposium, 174.

Geschwind N. "Behavioural changes in temporal lobe epilepsy". Psychol Med. 1979.

Gellhorn, E., Kiely, W.F. "Mystical states of consciousness: neurophysiological and clinical aspects." J Nerv Ment Dis. 1972;154:399-405.

Gilbert SL, Dobyns WB, Lahn BT (2005) Genetic links between brain development and brain evolution. Nat Rev Genet 6.

Gray JA. The Psychology of Fear and Stress. 2nd ed. New York, NY: Cambridge University Press; 1988.

Gloor, P. (1992), 'Amygdala and temporal lobe epilepsy', in The Amygdala: Neurobiological Aspects of Emotion, Memory and Mental Dysfunction, ed J.P. Aggleton (New York: Wiley-Liss).

Greenspan, S. I. and S. G. Shanker (2004). The first idea: How symbols, language, and intelligence evolved from our early primate ancestors to modern humans. Cambridge, MA: Da Capo Press.

Grady, D. (1993), 'The vision thing: Mainly in the brain', Discover, June.

Gallagher HL, Frith CD (2003) Functional imaging of 'theory of mind'. Trends Cogn Sci 7: 77.

Gallese V, Fogassi L, Fadiga L, Rizzolatti G (2002) Action representation and the inferior parietal lobule. In: Prinz W, Hommel B (eds) Attention & Performance XIX. Common mechanisms in perception and action. Oxford University Press, Oxford.

Gallese V, Keysers C, Rizzolatti G (2004) A unifying view of the basis of social cognition. Trends Cogn Sci 8: 396–403.

Gangitano M, Mottaghy FM, Pascual-Leone A (2001) Phase specific modulation of cortical motor output during movement observation. NeuroReport 12: 1489–1492.

Gangitano M, Mottaghy FM, Pascual-Leone A (2004) Modulation of premotor mirror neuron activity during observation of unpredictable grasping movements. Eur J Neurosci 20: 2193– 2202.

Goldman AI, Sripada CS (2004) Simulationist models of face-based emotion recognition. Cognition 94: 193–213.

Grèzes J, Costes N, Decety J (1998) Top-down effect of strategy on the perception of human biological motion: a PET investigation. Cogn Neuropsychol 15: 553–582.

Grèzes J, Armony JL, Rowe J, Passingham RE (2003) Activations related to "mirror" and "canonical" neurones in the human brain: an fMRI study. Neuroimage 18: 928–937.

Gross CG, Rocha-Miranda CE, Bender DB (1972) Visual properties of neurons in the inferotemporal cortex of the macaque. J Neurophysiol 35: 96–111.

Hari R, Forss N, Avikainen S, Kirveskari S, Salenius S, Rizzolatti G

(1998) Activation of human primary motor cortex during action observation: a neuromagnetic study. Proc. Natl Acad Sci USA 95: 15061–15065.

Hardy, G. H. (1940). Ramanujan. Cambridge: Cambridge University Press.

Hall, Daniel, Keith Meador, and Harold Koenig. "Measuring Religiousness in Health Research: Review and Critique." Journal of Religion and Health 47, no. 2 (2008)

Harris, Sam, Jonas Kaplan, Ashley Curiel, Susan Bookheimer, Marco Iacoboni, and Mark Cohen. "The Neural Correlates of Religious and Nonreligious Belief." PLoS One 4, no. 10 (October 1, 2009)

Halgren, E. (1992), 'Emotional neurophysiology of the amygdala within the context of human cognition', in The Amygdala:

Neurobiological Aspects of Emotion, Memory and Mental Dysfunction, ed J.P. Aggleton (New York: Wiley-Liss).

Halligan PW, Fink GR, Marshal JC, Vallar G. 2003. Spatial cognition: evidence from visual neglect. Trends Cogn Sci.

Handbook of Emotions, Edited by Michael Lewis, Jeannette M. Haviland-Jones, and Lisa Feldman Barrett, The Guilford Press; 3rd edition (2010).

Haggard, P., Clark, S. and Kalogeras,]. (2002) Voluntary action and conscious awareness, Nature Neuroscience 5, 382-5. Haggard, P., Newman, C. and Magno, E. (1999) On the perceived time of voluntary actions. British Journal of Psychology 90, 291-303.

Hameroff, S.R. and Penrose, R. (1996) Conscious events as orchestrated space-time selections. Journal of Consciousness Studies 3(1), 36-53; also reprinted in J. Shear (ed.) (1997)

Explaining Consciousness-The Hard Problem. Cambridge, MA, MIT Press, 177-95.

Hardcastle, V.G. (2000) How to understand theN in NCC. InT. Metzinger (ed.) Neural Correlates of Consciousness. Cambridge, MA, MIT Press, 259-64.

Harding, D.E. (1961) On Having no Head: Zen and the Re-Discovery of the Obvious. London, Buddhist Society.

Hardy, A. (1979) The Spiritual Nature of Man: A Study of Contemporary Religious Experience. Oxford, Clarendon Press.

Hamad, S. (1990) The symbol grounding problem. Physica D 42, 335-46.

Hamad, S. (2001) No easy way out. The Sciences 41(2), 36-42.

Harre, R. and Gillett, G. (1994) The Discursive Mind. Thousand Oaks, CA, Sage.

Haugeland, J. (ed.) (1997) Mind Design II: Philosophy, Psychology, Artificial Intelligence. Cambridge, MA, MIT Press.

Hauser, M.D. (2000) Wild Minds: What Animals Really Think. New York, Henry Holt and Co.; London, Penguin.

Hearne, K. (1990) The Dream Machine. Northants, Aquarian.

Hebb, D.O. (1949) The Organization of Behavior. New York, Wiley.

Helmholtz, H.L.F. von (1856-67) Treatise on Physiological Optics.

Hess, EH (1975) "The role of pupil size in communication," Scientific American, 233(5), 110–12.

Heyes, C.M. (1998) Theory of mind in nonhuman primates. Behavioral and

Brain Sciences 21, 101-48; with commentaries.

Heyes, C.M. and Galef, B.G. (eds) (1996) Social Learning in Animals: The Roots of Culture. San Diego, CA, Academic Press.

Hilgard, E.R. (1986) Divided Consciousness: Multiple Controls in Human Thought and Action. New York, Wiley.

Hitler, Adolf. Mein Kampf, 1925

Hodgson, R. (1891) A case of double consciousness. Proceedings of the Society for Psychical Research 7, 221-58.

Hofstadter, D.R. and Dennett, D.C. (eds) (1981) The Mind's I: Fantasies and Reflections on Self and Soul. London, Penguin.

Holland, J. (ed.) (2001) Ecstasy: The Complete Guide: A Comprehensive Look at the Risks and Benefits of

MDMA. Rochester, VT, Park Street Press.

Holmes, D.S. (1987) The influence of meditation versus rest on physiological arousal. In M. West (ed.) The Psychology of Meditation. Oxford, Clarendon Press, 81-103.

Holmstrom, David. 1992, Christian Science Monitor

Holt, J. (1999) Blindsight in debates about qualia. Journal of Consciousness Studies 6(5), 54-71.

Horgan, J. (1994), 'Can science explain consciousness?', Scientific American, 271.

Holloway RL (1996) Evolution of the human brain. In: Lock A, Peters CR (eds) Handbook of human symbolic evolution. Oxford University Press, Oxford

Iacoboni M, Woods RP, Brass M, Bekkering H, Mazziotta JC, Rizzolatti

G (1999) Cortical mechanisms of human imitation. Science 286: 2526–2528.

Iacoboni M, Koski LM, Brass M, Bekkering H, Woods RP, Dubeau MC, Mazziotta JC, Rizzolatti G (2001) Reafferent copies of imitated actions in the right superior temporal cortex. Proc Natl Acad Sci USA 98: 13995–13999.

Jeannerod M (1988) The neural and behavioural organization of goal-directed movements. Clarendon Press, Oxford.

Johnson-Frey SH, Maloof FR, Newman-Norlund R, Farrer C, Inati S, Grafton ST (2003) Actions or hand-objects interactions? Human inferior frontal cortex and action observation. Neuron 39: 1053–1058.

Jackson, F. (1982) Epiphenomenal qualia. Philosophical Quarterly 32, 127-36.

James, W. (1890) The Principles of Psychology (2 volumes). London, Macmillan.

James, W. (1902) The Varieties of Religious Experience: A Study in Human Nature. New York and London, Longmans, Green and Co.

Jansen, K. (2001) Ketamine: Dreams and Realities. Sarasota, FL, Multidisciplinary Association for Psychedelic Studies.

Jay, M. (ed.) (1999) Artificial Paradises: A Drugs Reader. London, Penguin.

Jaynes, J. (1976) The Origin of Consciousness in the Breakdown of the Bicameral Mind. New York, Houghton Mifflin.

Johnson, M.K. and Raye, C.L. (1981) Reality monitoring. Psychological Review 88, 67-85.

Kadim I, Mahgoub O, Baqir S et al. (2015) Cultured meat from muscle stem cells: a review of challenges and prospects. J Integr Agr 14: 222–233

Koski L, Iacoboni M, Dubeau MC, Woods RP, Mazziotta JC (2003) Modulation of cortical activity during different imitative behaviors. J Neurophysiol 89: 460–471.

Krolak-Salmon P, Henaff MA, Isnard J, Tallon-Baudry C, Guenot M, Vighetto A, Bertrand O, Mauguiere F (2003) An attention modulated response to disgust in human ventral anterior insula. Ann Neurol 53: 446–453.

Kandel, E. R. In Search of Memory: The Emergence of a New Science of Mind, W. W. Norton & Company (2007).

Kandel E. R. Schwartz JH, Jessel TM. Principles of neural sciences. New York; McGraw Hill, 2000.

Kanizsa, G. (1979), Organization In Vision (New York: Praeger).

Kaloupek DG, Scott JR, Khatami V. Assessment of coping strategies associated with syncope in blood donors. J Psychosom Res. 1985;29:207-214.

Kanwisher, N. (2001) Neural events and perceptual awareness. Cognition 79, 89-113; also reprinted inS. Dehaene (ed.) The Cognitive Neuroscience of Consciousness. Cambridge, MA, MIT Press, 89-113.

Kapleau, Roshi P. (1980) The Three Pillars of Zen: Teaching, Practice, and Enlightenment (revised edn). New York, Doubleday.

Karn, K. and Hayhoe, M. (2000) Memory representations guide targeting eye movements in a natural task. Visual Cognition 7, 673-703.

Kasamatsu, A. and Hirai, T. (1966) An electroencephalographic study on the Zen meditation (zazen). Folia

Psychiatrica et Neurologica Japonica 20, 315-36.

Kaiserman-Abramof, I. R., Graybiel, A. M., & Nauta, W. J. (1980). The thalamic projection to cortical area 17 in a congenitally anophthalmic mouse strain. Neuroscience, 5, 41–52.

Kanold, P. O., Kara, P., Reid, R. C., & Shatz, C. J. (2003). Role of subplate neurons in functional maturation of visual cortical columns. Science, 301, 521–525.

Kennedy, H., & Dehay, C. (1988). Functional implications of the anatomical organization of the callosal projections of visual areas V1 and V2 in the macaque monkey. Behav. Brain Res., 29, 225–236.

Kentridge, R.W. and Heywood, C.A. (1999) The status of blindsight. Journal of Consciousness Studies 6(5), 3-11.

Kihlstrom, J.F. (1996) Perception without awareness of what is perceived, learning without awareness of what is learned. In M. Velmans (ed.) The Science of Consciousness. London, Routledge, 23-46.

Kollerstrom, N. (1999) The path of Halley's comet, and Newton's late apprehension of the law of gravity. Annals of Science 56, 331-56.

Kosslyn, S.M. (1980) Image and Mind. Cambridge, MA, Harvard University Press.

Kosslyn, S.M. (1988) Aspects of a cognitive neuroscience of mental imagery. Science 240, 1621-6.

Kinsbourne, M. (1995), 'The intralaminar thalamic nucleii', Consciousness and Cognition, 4.

Kjaer, Troels, Camilla Bertelsen, Paola Piccini, David Brooks, Jorgen Alving, and Hans Lou. "Increased Dopamine Tone during Meditation- Induced Change of Consciousness." Cognitive Brain Research 13, no. 2 (April 2002)

Kölmel HW. 1985. Complex visual hallucinations in the hemianopic field. J Neurol Neurosurg Psychiatry.

Koenig, Harold. "Research on Religion, Spirituality, and Mental Health: A Review." Canadian Journal of Psychiatry 54, no. 5 (May 2009)

Koenig, Harold, ed. Handbook of Religion and Mental Health. San Diego, CA: Academic Press, 1998

Kraepelin E. Psychiatry: A Textbook for Students and Physicians. New York, NY: Science History Publications; 1990.

Lauglin, Charles, John McManus, and Eugene d'Aquili. Brain, Symbol, and Experience. 2nd ed. New York: Columbia University Press, 1992

Lakoff, G. and M. Johnson (1999). Philosophy in the flesh. Basic Books: New York.

LeDoux, J. E. (1996). The emotional brain. New York: Simon & Schuster.

LeDoux, J.E. (1992), 'Emotion and the amygdala', in The Amygdala: Neurobiological Aspects of Emo- tion, Memory and Mental Dysfunction, ed J.P. Aggleton (New York: Wiley-Liss).

Levin, D.T. and Simons, D.J. (1997) Failure to detect changes to attended objects in motion pictures. Psychonomic Bulletin and Review 4, 501-6.

Levine,J. (1983) Materialism and qualia: the explanatory gap. Pacific Philosophical Quarterly 64, 354-61.

Levine,J. (2001) Purple Haze: The Puzzle of Consciousness. New York, Oxford University Press. Levine, S. (1979) A Gradual Awakening. New York, Doubleday.

Levinson, B.W. (1965) States of awareness during general anaesthesia.

British Journal of Anaesthesia 37, 544-6.

Lewicki, P., Czyzewska, M. and Hoffman, H. (1987) Unconscious acquisition of complex procedural knowledge. Journal of Experimental Psychology: Learning, Memory and Cognition 13, 523-30.

Lewicki, P., Hill, T. and Bizot, E. (1988) Acquisition of procedural knowledge about a pattern of stimuli that cannot be articulated. Cognitive Psychology 20, 24-37.

Lewicki, P., Hill, T. and Czyzewska, M. (1992) Nonconscious acquisition of information. American Psychologist 47, 796-801.

Manthey S, Schubotz RI, von Cramon DY (2003). Premotor cortex in observing erroneous action: an fMRI study. Brain Res Cogn Brain Res 15: 296–307.

Mesulam MM, Mufson EJ (1982) Insula of the old world monkey. III: Efferent cortical output and comments on function. J Comp Neurol 212: 38–52.

Naskar, Abhijit. "Homo: A Brief History of Consciousness", 2015

Naskar, Abhijit. "What is Mind?", 2016

Naskar, Abhijit. "Love, God & Neurons: Memoir of A Scientist who found himself by getting lost", 2016

Naskar, Abhijit. "Principia Humanitas", 2017

Naskar, Abhijit. "We Are All Black: A Treatise on Racism", 2017

Naskar, Abhijit. "Either Civilized or Phobic: A Treatise on Homosexuality", 2017

Naskar, Abhijit. "I Am The Thread: My Mission", 2017

Naskar, Abhijit. "The Bengal Tigress: A Treatise on Gender Equality", 2017

Naskar, Abhijit. "Morality Absolute", 2017

Naskar, Abhijit. "Build Bridges not Walls: In the name of Americana", 2018

Naskar, Abhijit. "Fabric of Humanity", 2018

Naskar, Abhijit. "Lives To Serve Before I Sleep", 2019

Naskar, Abhijit. "Citizens of Peace: Beyond the Savagery of Sovereignty", 2019

Naskar, Abhijit. "The Constitution of The United Peoples of Earth", 2019

Naskar, Abhijit. "Neurons Giveth, Neurons Taketh Away | Abhijit Naskar | TEDxIIMRanchi", 2019 https://www.youtube.com/watch?v=BNX-Q0ySm80

Naskar, Abhijit. "Mission Reality", 2019

Naskar, Abhijit. "Operation Justice: To Make A Society That Needs No Law", 2019

Naskar, Abhijit. "Every Generation Needs Caretakers: The Gospel of Patriotism", 2020

Naskar, Abhijit. "Hurricane Humans: Give me accountability, I'll give you peace", 2020

Naskar, Abhijit. "Revolution Indomable", 2020

Naskar, Abhijit. "Servitude is Sanctitude", 2020

Naskar, Abhijit. "Good Scientist: When Science and Service Combine", 2020

Newberg, Andrew, and Jeremy Iversen. "The Neural Basis of the Complex Mental Task of Meditation: Neurotransmitter and Neurochemical Considerations." Medical Hypotheses 61, no. 2 (2003).

Newberg, Andrew. "How God Changes Your Brain: An Introduction to Jewish Neurotheology", CCAR Journal: The Reform Jewish Quarterly, Winter 2016.

Newberg, Andrew, and Stephanie Newberg. "A Neuropsychological Perspective on Spiritual Development." In Handbook of Spiritual Development in Childhood and Adolescence, edited by Eugene Roehlkepartain, Pamela King, Linda Wagener, and Peter Benson. London: Sage Publications, Inc., 2005

Newberg, Andrew. "The Neurotheology Link An Intersection Between Spirituality and Health", Alternative and Complimentary Therapies, Vol 21 No 1, February 2015.

Newberg, Andrew, Nancy Wintering, Dharma Khalsa, Hannah Roggenkamp, and Mark Waldman. "Meditation Effects on Cognitive Function and Cerebral Blood Flow in

Subjects with Memory Loss: A Preliminary Study." Journal of Alzheimer's Disease 20, no. 2 (2010)

Nash, M. (1995), 'Glimpses of the mind', Time.

Nesse RM. Proximate and evolutionary studies of anxiety, stress and depression: synergy at the interface. Neurosci Biobehav Rev. 1999;23:895-903.

Nicolelis, Miguel. (2011) "Beyond Boundaries: The New Neuroscience of Connecting Brains with Machines--- and How It Will Change Our Lives", Times Books

O'Hara, K. and Scutt, T. (1996) There is no hard problem of consciousness. Journal of Consciousness Studies 3(4), 290-302, reprinted in J. Shear (ed.) (1997) Explaining Consciousness. Cambridge, MA, MIT Press, 69-82.

O'Regan, J.K. (1992) Solving the "real" mysteries of visual perception: the world as an outside memory. Canadian Journal of Psychology 46, 461-88.

O'Regan, J.K. and Noe, A. (2001) A sensorimotor account of vision and visual consciousness. Behavioral and Brain Sciences 24(5), 883-917.

O'Regan, J.K., Rensink, R.A. and Clark,].]. (1999) Change-blindness as a result of "mudsplashes." Nature 398, 34.

Ornstein, R.E. (1977) The Psychology of Consciousness (2nd edn). New York, Harcourt.

Ornstein, R.E. (1986) The Psychology of Consciousness (3rd edn). New York, Pehguin.

Ornstein, R.E. (1992) The Evolution of Consciousness. New York, Touchstone.

Penfield W, Faulk ME (1955) The insula: further observations on its function. Brain 78: 445– 470.

Penrose, R. (1994), Shadows of the Mind (Oxford: Oxford University Press).

Penrose, R. (1989), The Emperor's New Mind: Concerning Computers, Minds and The Laws of Physics (Oxford: Oxford University Press).

Persinger, "'I would kill in God's name' role of sex, weekly church attendance, report of a religious experience and limbic lability" Perceptual and Motor Skills 1997.

Persinger "Experimental simulation of the God experience" Neurotheology 2003.

Persinger, M. A. (1993b). Personality changes following brain injury as a grief response to the loss of sense of self: Phenomenological themes as indices of local lability and neurocognitive restructuring as psycho- therapy. Psychological Reports, 72

Persinger, Corradini, Clement, Keaney, et al "Neurotheology and its convergence with neuroquantology" NeuroQuantology 2010.

Persinger, Koren and St-Pierre "The electromagnetic induction of mystical and altered states within the laboratory" Journal of Consciousness Exploration and Research 2010.

Persinger "Case report: A prototypical spontaneous 'sensed presence' of a sentient being and concomitant electroencephalographic activity in the clinical laboratory" Neurocase 2008.

Persinger and Saroka "Potential production of Hughlings Jackson's "parasitic consciousness" by physiologically-patterned weak transcerebral magnetic fields: QEEG and source localization" Epilepsy & Behavior 28 (2013).

Persinger. "The neuropsychiatry of paranormal experiences". J Neuropsychiatry Clin Neurosci 2001.

Persinger. "Neuropsychological bases of god beliefs", New York: Praeger, 1987

Persinger. "Temporal lobe epileptic signs and correlative behaviors displayed by normal populations", Journal of General Psychology, 1986

Perry BD, Pollard R. Homeostasis, stress, trauma, and adaptation. A neurodevelopmental view of childhood trauma. Child Adolesc Psychiatr Clin N Am. 1998;7:33.

Paré, D. & Llinás, R. (1995), 'Conscious and preconscious processes as seen from the standpoint of sleep-waking cycle neurophysiology', Neuropsychologia, 33.

P. S. de Laplace. Essai Philosophique sur les Probabilites [1814], in Academy des Sciences, Oeuvres Complotes de Laplace, Vol. 7, Gauthier-Villars, Paris (1886).

Perrett DI, Harries MH, Bevan R, Thomas S, Benson PJ, Mistlin AJ, Chitty AJ, Hietanen JK, Ortega JE (1989) Frameworks of analysis for the neural representation of animate objects and actions. J Exp Bio 146: 87–113.

Phillips ML, Young AW, Senior C, Brammer M, Andrew C, Calder AJ, Bullmore ET, Perrett DI, Rowland D, Williams SC, Gray JA, David AS (1997) A specific neural substrate for perceiving facial expressions of disgust. Nature 389: 495–498.

Phillips ML, Young AW, Scott SK, Calder AJ, Andrew C, Giampietro V, Williams SC, Bullmore ET, Brammer M, Gray JA (1998) Neural responses to facial and vocal expressions of fear and disgust. Proc R Soc Lond B Biol Sci 265: 1809–1817.

Puce A, Perrett D (2003) Electrophysiological and brain imaging of biological motion. Philosoph Trans Royal Soc Lond, Series B, 358: 435–445.

Ramachandran VS. Behavioral and magnetoencephalographic correlates of plasticity in the adult human brain. Proc Natl Acad Sci USA 1993; 90: 10413–20.

Ramachandran VS. Phantom limbs, neglect syndromes, repressed memories, and Freudian psychology. Int Rev Neurobiol 1994; 37: 291–333.

Ramachandran VS. Plasticity and functional recovery in neurology. Clin Med 2005; 5: 368–73.

Ramachandran VS, Hirstein W. The perception of phantom limbs. The D. O. Hebb lecture. Brain 1998; 121: 1603–30.

Ramachandran VS, Rogers-Ramachandran D, Cobb S. Touching the phantom limb. Nature 1995; 377: 489–90.

Ramachandran VS, Rogers-Ramachandran D. Phantom limbs and neural plasticity. Arch Neurol 2000; 57: 317–20.

Ramachandran VS, Rogers-Ramachandran D. It's all done with mirrors. Sci Am Mind 2007; 18: 16–9.

Ramachandran VS, Rogers-Ramachandran D. Sensations referred to a patient's phantom arm from another subjects intact arm: perceptual correlates of mirror neurons. Med Hypotheses 2008; 70: 1233–4.

Ramachandran VS, Rogers-Ramachandran D, Stewart M. Perceptual correlates of massive cortical reorganization. Science 1992; 258: 1159–60.

Rizzolatti G, Craighero L (2004) The mirror-neuron system. Annu Rev Neurosci 27: 169–192.

Rizzolatti G, Fogassi L, Gallese V (2001) Neurophysiological mechanisms underlying the understanding and imitation of action. Nature Rev Neurosci 2:661–670.

Rock I, Victor J. Vision and touch: an experimentally created conflict between the two senses. Science 1964; 143: 594–6.

Rose´n B, Lundborg G. Training with a mirror in rehabilitation of the hand. Scand J Plast Reconstr Surg Hand Surg 2005; 39: 104–8.

Royet JP, Plailly J, Delon-Martin C, Kareken DA, Segebarth C (2003) fMRI of emotional responses to odors: influence of hedonic valence and judgment, handedness, and gender. Neuroimage 20: 713–728.

Rozin R Haidt J and McCauley CR (2000) Disgust. In: Lewis M, Haviland-Jones JM (eds) Handbook of Emotion. 2nd Edition. Guilford Press, New York, pp 637–653.

Saxe R, Carey S, Kanwisher N (2004) Understanding other minds: linking developmental psychology and functional neuroimaging. Annu Rev Psychol 55: 87–124.

S. J. Russell and P. Norvig, Artificial intelligence: a modern approach (3rd edition): Prentice Hall, 2009.

Schienle A, Stark R, Walter B, Blecker C, Ott U, Kirsch P, Sammer G, Vaitl D (2002) The insula is not specifically involved in disgust processing: an fMRI study. Neuroreport 13: 2023–2026.

Showers MJC, Lauer EW (1961) Somatovisceral motor patterns in the insula. J Comp Neurol 117: 107–115.

Singer T, Seymour B, O'Doherty J, Kaube H, Dolan RJ, Frith CD (2004) Empathy for pain involves the affective but not the sensory components of pain. Science 303: 1157–1162.

Smith A (1759) The theory of moral sentiments (ed. 1976). Clarendon Press, Oxford.

S. N. Bose (1924). "Plancks Gesetz und Lichtquantenhypothese". Zeitschrift für Physik. 26 (1): 178–181.

Sprengelmeyer R, Rausch M, Eysel UT, Przuntek H (1998) Neural structures associated with recognition of facial expressions of basic emotions Proc R Soc Lond B Biol Sci 265: 1927–1931.

Strafella AP, Paus T (2000) Modulation of cortical excitability during action observation: a transcranial magnetic stimulation study. NeuroReport 11: 2289–2292.

Schilling, Vincent. 2017, indian country today

Stein, Stephen K. 2017, The Sea in World History: Exploration, Travel, and Trade

Simonsen R (2015) Eating for the future: veganism and the challenge of in vitro meat. In: Stapleton P, Byers A (Hg). Biopolitics and utopia. Palgrave Macmillan, New York (2015), S 167–190

Tanaka K (1996) Inferotemporal cortex and object vision. Ann Rev Neurosci. 19: 109–140.

Tesla N. "My Inventions", 1919

T. R. Society, "Machine learning: the power and promise of computers that learn by example," ed. The Royal Society, 2017.

Tomasello M, Call J (1997) Primate cognition. Oxford University Press, Oxford.

Tremblay C, Robert M, Pascual-Leone A, Lepore F, Nguyen DK, Carmant L, Bouthillier A, Theoret H (2004) Action observation and execution: intracranial recordings in a human subject. Neurology. 63: 937–938.

Umilta MA, Kohler E, Gallese V, Fogassi L, Fadiga L, Keysers C, Rizzolatti G (2001) "I know what you are doing": a neurophysiological study. Neuron 32: 91–101.

Von Wright G.H., (1963), Norm and Action. A Logical Inquiry, Routledge & Kegan Paul, London.

Von Wright G.H., (1976), "Determinism and the Study of Man", in Essays on Explanation and Understanding, ed. by J. Manninen and R. Tuomela, Reidel, Dordrecht.

Von Wright G.H., (1977), "What is Humanism?", The Lindlay Lecture, University of Arkansas, Lawrence, Kansas.

Von Wright G.H., (1979), "Humanism and the Humanities", in Philosophy and Grammar, ed. by S. Kanger and S. Öhman, Reidel, Dordrecht, pp. 1-16. Reprinted in von Wright (1993).

Von Wright G.H., (1980), Freedom and Determination, North-Holland Publishing Co., Amsterdam.

Von Wright G.H., (1985), Of Human Freedom, The Tanner Lectures on Human Values,

Vol. VI, ed. by S. M. McMurrin, University of Utah Press, Salt Lake City, pp. 107-70. Reprinted in von Wright (1998).

Von Wright G.H., (1993), The Tree of Knowledge and Other Essays, Brill, Leiden.

Von Wright G.H., (1997), "Progress: Fact and Fiction", in The Idea of Progress, ed. by A. Burgen et al., W. de Gruyter, Berlin, pp. 1-18.

Von Wright G.H., (1998), In the Shadow of Descartes: Essays in the Philosophy of Mind, Kluwer, Dordrecht.